CATS IN SWEATERS

CATS IN SWEATERS

JONAH STERN

Brimming with creative inspiration, how-to projects, and useful information to enrich your everyday life, Quarto Knows is a favorite destination for those pursuing their interests and passions. Visit our site and dig deeper with our books into your area of interest: Quarto Creates, Quarto Cooks, Quarto Homes, Quarto Lives, Quarto Drives, Quarto Explores, Quarto Gifts, or Quarto Kids.

Photography: Heather's Photography and Richie Schwartz
All other photographs © Shutterstock
Book Interior Design: Monica Gurevich-Importico
Senior Design Manager: Heidi North
Wardrobe: Kimberly Kindelsperger

This edition published in 2019 by Crestline, an imprint of
The Quarto Group 142 West 36th Street, 4th Floor New York, NY 10018 USA
T (212) 779-4972 **F** (212) 779-6058 **www.QuartoKnows.com**

First published in 2016 by Rock Point, an imprint of The Quarto Group,
142 West 36th Street, 4th Floor, New York, NY 10018, USA

Crestline titles are also available at discount for retail, wholesale, promotional, and bulk purchase. For details, contact the Special Sales Manager by email at specialsales@quarto.com or by mail at The Quarto Group, Attn: Special Sales Manager, 100 Cummings Center, Suite 265-D, Beverly, MA 01915, USA.

10 9 8 7 6 5 4 3 2 1

ISBN: 978-0-7858-3773-2

Printed in China

CONTENTS

KITTIES GETTING SNUGGLY

Danger! Stand back!

These kitties are so cute they will destroy you with extremely tender nuzzles, smooches, and kneads. You'll hate to give in, but surrendering to the sweetness and snuggles is your only choice.

"I actually like being in charge of employee birthday parties, staff spirit awards, and cleaning out the work refrigerator." #marthastewartrules

FUN FACT: *President of the Ed Sheeran fan club*

Despite a black belt in karate and a king's wardrobe of bedazzled sweaters, this tender tiger can cuddle, snuggle, and wrap you in a hug before you can say "Suspicious Minds." #elvis4evr

NICKNAME: *Hunk O'Love*

NAME: Rose

"When I close my eyes, there's always more room on that wooden plank. Are you photographing me like one of those French girls?" #luvleo

FAVORITE MOVIE: Titanic

NAME: Oliver

When he's not busy dishing up the hottest gossip on all your favorite celebrities or watching *E! News*, Oliver is great at saying things better left unsaid and being your best friend at a party. #bravoaddict

CAT-CHPHRASE: "If you can't say something nice about someone, come sit next to me."

15

NAME: Moonshine

"Mom, can I be your pocket panther?" #momsrule

FAVORITE SONG: The Weeknd's "I Can't Feel My Face"

NAME: Snowy

"Just because you're wearing a sweater doesn't mean you can slouch on glamour."
#hotdudeswearingsweaters

FAVORITE SONG: Jidenna's "Classic Man"

NAME: **Willie**

He lettered in tennis and performing arts and has the varsity sweater to prove it. This handsome guy has a sensitive side and enjoys spicy Thai food and fashion week. #perfectman

LOVES: *Disney, Michael Jackson, and my two dads*

NAME: **Tigger**

This whiskered one is ready for the snuggle struggle: a romance, bromance, or maybe just a long nap on your lap. #sensitivesweetheart

LOVES: *Hummus and binging on Dancing with the Stars.*

NAME: *Leroy*

Like a boss, Leroy lets you know when you're fabulous, hilarious, and generally pushing the limits of awesome. #turnup

FUN FACT: **I'm a fiery Aries looking for that one special lucky Libra.**

24

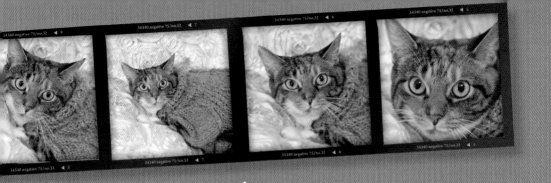

NAME: **Fang**

"Though I enjoy wearing fur year round, I really look forward to sweater weather." #fluffeh

FAVORITE FOOD: **Pumpkin mug cakes**

The ever-romantic Ivy knows that wearing a conversation piece, like this adorable flower brooch, makes her more approachable at parties or when she's in the waiting room at the vet. #sweetie

FAVORITE MOVIE: **The Notebook**

DIVA CATS:

Ladylike Sweeties

Is it hot in here or are these cats
just looking incredible?

With their big dreams, inventive looks, and queen-size
swagger, our posse of flossy felines are stylin' out!

NAME: Zooey

Bless her heart, Little Miss Zooey just pitches a fit if things aren't just so. Now hush your mouth, come over here, and give this darlin' some sugar. #southernbelle

CAT-CHPHRASE: **"Well butter my buns and call me a biscuit!"**

NAME: Topaz

Every girl wants to be her, and every guy wants to be with her. She may not be Taylor Swift but Topaz is close enough. #squadgoals

LOVES: Paris, soft blankets, and gelato

NAME: *Belle*

Dontcha know, if Belle had her druthers, she'd be serving up a delicious tater tot hotdish before you could say "malarkey." #midwestgirl

FUN FACT: *Great pleasure can be found in butter sculptures and large glasses of milk.*

NAME: *Lady*

She may show up fifteen minutes late with a green juice, but Lady has some questions. Let's get real and talk about your feelings—and where did you get that jacket? #girlfriendsrule

FAVORITE MOVIE: *Bridesmaids*

NAME: Jade

Did somebody say casual Friday? Not this lady. Jade is a chic lady who knows the power of accessorizing. #whoworeitbetter

CAT-CHPHRASE: "When I woke up this morning, I had no plans on looking this good."

NAME: **Ivy**

At times more daring than graceful, Ivy's sitting pretty here, as delicate as a flower (if only for a second). #cutepetclub

FAVORITE CHARACTER: *Sally in The Nightmare Before Christmas*

NAME: Dee-Dee

A strong woman and just about as close to purrrrfection as you can get, Dee-Dee also looks good. I mean really good. #whorunstheworld

FAVORITE SONG: Selena Gomez's "Same Old Love"

44

NAME: Codie

Unafraid to get in touch with her inner fashionista, Codie enjoys shopping for vintage clothes and drinking herbal tea. #grrrls

FAVORITE TV SHOW: Portlandia

This elegant kitteh would never wear white after Labor Day nor have a phone convo while ordering her half-caf latte. Madison is a first-class lady who always knows about the latest restaurant and has tickets to the hottest show. #ladylike

CAT-CHPHRASE: "**Manhattan is the only place for me.**"

NAME: Riley

When she isn't shaking the walls with her purrs,

Riley's favorite things are:

1. Leg warmers

2. Melted cheese

3. Chin rubs that last at least five minutes

FAVORITE MOVIE: *Pitch Perfect*

NAME: *Gina*

Stuck in a rut? Let this party animal take you on a magical journey where pouncing occurs daily and Urban Outfitters has a sweater department for cats. #socute

IDOL: *Christina Hendricks*

SILLY SWEATERS

✦ 🐾 ✦

*Raise you paws, claws, and whiskers 'cause
it's about to get ridiculous!*

These mad mousers have their unflinching gazes set
to stir-crazy. Try not to crack as these silly kitties
are ready to seize the moment, execute a surprise ninja
attack, or dress up as your favorite cupcake.

NAME: *Buddy*

"I may not always play with my toy lobster, but when I do it'll be on your bed at 4 a.m." #bostonboy

CAT-CHPHRASE: **"I'm frickin' awesome and so is my pet lobstah."**

57

NAME: Claude

This kitty-cat superhero is here to save you from empty laps and lame parties. When he's not hurling hairballs at the bad guys, he is busy resisting Kitty Kryptonite aka whipped cream. #dccomicsrule

FUN FACT: Has a secret membership to the Wonder Woman fan club

NAME: **Topaz**

This picture-perfect Pinterest dessert is the cutest cupcake you'll ever find. Ready to decorate with mason jars and DIY your wedding, Topaz is a pretty pinner looking for love amongst the crumbs. #pinterestgrl

CAT-CHPHRASE: *"All good things come with sprinkles!"*

NAME: **Madison**

Owning the bumblebee look the way a true Beyoncé fan should, this girl runs the world. #putaringonit

CAT-CHPHRASE: "Yaaas Queen Bey!"

NAME: *Buddy aka Adorablesaurus*

It's hard to have a proper sense of danger when your predator purrs. #cattitudeclub

FAVORITE MOVIE: *Jurassic World*

She's fancy, fresh, and ready to hang…all the better to be your Bun Bun. #bunnylove

FUN FACT: "Tacocat" spelled backward is…

There are millions of fish in the sea; however, purrmaids are rare. This magical creature fills the ocean with purrs and is easily spotted near food bowls and sunny windows. #dreamcometrue

FAVORITE MOVIE: **Splash**

When she falls in love, it will be forever. This elegant sweetheart loves long naps in the sunshine, cream cheese, and has also been known to give you that "Where have you been all day?" look. #mrdarcy

FAVORITE MOVIE: *Pride and Prejudice*

HOLIDAY SWEATERS

❄

They aren't just a holiday tradition for people.

These kitties are joining in the fun. Cats are partying like animals in festive holiday sweaters.

NAME: **Finnegan**

Finnegan is contemplating his future: Is it full of fluffy love or fleek knitwear? More money and more problems? He's learning how to appreciate the little things. #gratitude

CAT-CHPHRASE: **"When I get worried I just ask myself, 'What would Oprah do?'"**

NAME: Whispers

Shy girl Whispers is no shrinking violet at the holiday party, and she's a star at the annual cookie swap with her sparkling ginger chip cookies. #christmasgrl

CAT-CHPHRASE: "A cookie a day keeps the sadness away."

NAME: *Nikko*

Smart and serious, Nikko is ready to have a Starbucks peppermint latte and discuss the *New York Times* op-ed page. In his downtime, he's all about *Game of Thrones*. #nyhipster

FAVORITE SONG: *Anything on vinyl*

NAME: **Modigliani and Marcello**

Things these twins enjoy doing together: cuddling, being cute, wearing sweaters, meowing, everything. #twinning

FAVORITE SONG: *Brenda Lee's "Rockin' Around the Christmas Tree"*

CATS WITHOUT SWEATERS

Surprisingly, sweaters aren't for everyone. We love these independent felines regardless. #freetobeme